MOTOWN, HOW DID IT OPERATE?

(A Much Closer Look at Motown)

PW Williams

First Edition: July 2024

ISBN: 9798893971248

Published by AMZ Kindle Direct Publications

DEDICATION

To my Mom

And to the Artist of Motown, who has passed on and left many memories of the fabulous music of all times.

ACKNOWLEDGMENT

My Lord and God Jesus Christ first

My Mom for her insight because she revealed my talent to me at nine years old: my ability to write songs, play the piano, sing any key, and harmonize. Everyone can't do that. Harmony was special.

Thank you, the public, for choosing my book hope you enjoy the reading and information of the past.

In addition, Berry Gordy shared information through archives. Smokey Robinson shares his views regarding the History of Motown. Harvey Fuqua, Eddie Kendricks, Mary Wilson and a host of others.

First, praise God and his Son, our Lord, the wonderful and magnificent Jesus Christ. Bless this book.

I have been in the music world for over 50 years. I am a retired singer and writer-producer. I have listened to various kinds of music all my life.

Back in the early 1960s, I heard people say Motown this and Motown that, and my curiosity started running wild.

What is Motown? And who is Motown? Every day, I started looking into Motown. I was surprised because the person who was called Motown was a man. I will call him Berry, like the kind you eat. Berry used to be a boxer. I found out that did not work out, so he quit. In addition, he was a factory worker; he moved on to open a music store selling records and albums. The problem was that the public wanted to buy blues music then; they did not want jazz music, and it did not work, so he lost the business. Berry had a writing talent, and he was exceptionally good at it. Berry also had sisters who were writers. Berry wrote for a singer named Jackie Wilson. This singer was hot in the market. Jackie Wilson was on another label, Brunswick (the label was referred to as a record company), Motown label, Brunswick label, etc. Everything Berry tried to do in the past did not work; he was a failure. All that is going to change.

So, he got a loan from his family. Berry was only 29 years old at that time. He opened his own record company. That was January 12, 1959; it was called Tamla Records. When anyone opens a record company, they need artists, meaning singers. Back then, when you auditioned to gain a singing contract, you did it live right there on the spot. A singer named Marvin Earl Johnson had a recording on a different label. But Berry heard it like the sound of Marv's voice. They worked out a deal, and Marv Johnson was the first singer (artist) to sing on the new label. It was Tamla Records, owned by Berry. The song was recorded in 1958. The Motown label was not established yet; the song was called Come to Me by Marv Johnson. You need a distributor for your record to be heard all over the country or try to distribute for local areas. The distributor gets your recording in stores on the radio in different states or all the states, plus internationally. For his small company, Tamla Records, Berry used a large record company with a large distributor; in other words, he sent his recording through the larger company. A deal between Berry and the large company.

The problem is when a singer goes through a big record company and cannot make it on the charts or give a hit. You make no money from your sales. When you hear the saying 'did the singer chart', what does that mean? It means there are 500 hundred slots on this chart.

The Billboard is a magazine that makes up this chart. It rates the record. The demand, airplay, and sales are guidelines to get on the chart.

If your record is #500 on the chart, you have a long way to go but at least you are on the chart.

When your record is #1 you are in demand by the public, in addition, the record company and you are making money, and the public wants to see and hear you. The top 20 on the chart are fabulous. If your recording is in the top 100 spot, that is great too.

Berry had money coming from his writing for Jackie Wilson plus money from some artists that made number 1 on the chart and number 2 in the country. His first #1 hit for the company was the Marvelettes Mr. Postman. They were right out of high school. Other recordings such as Don't mess with bill, Forever, Locking up My Heart. By the way, Marvin Gaye was playing the drums on Mr. Postman. The second hit was by the Miracles. Let me tell you a story about that second hit. The song was Shop Around. When Smokey and his group recorded that song, everyone said it was great, meaning Smokey and his group. But Berry had second thoughts later. So, Berry contacted Smokey and the rest of the group at about 3 am and told them to come to the recording studio A to re-record Shop Around. Berry said it was just too slow and the temple was not right. Everyone showed up at the recording studio except the piano player. Berry said to Smokey we have to record the song a little faster, so Berry had to play the piano because the piano player never showed. Shop Around became the company's very first million seller, it was #1 on the R&B chart and #2 on the POP chart (What does POP music mean? It is an Abbreviation that means popular, a contemporary type of music; some songs reach out to a few people, but popular music reaches out and appeals to a wide audience. Also, mainstream radio stations in various countries where Pop music is known as cross-over music because it appeals to another type of audience.) Shop Around became a national hit. Smokey and the Miracle's first recording with Tamla was called I Got a Job, the silhouettes were another group that had a #1 hit in the nation called Get a Job. So, Smokey wrote the answer to the song I Got a Job. The Silhouettes were with another label, not Tamla. Speaking of Smokey Robinson, let me tell you why his name is Smokey. I know Smokey personally. When Smokey was about 4 or 5 years old, he had an uncle who took Smokey to the movies. Smokey loved cowboys, especially singing cowboys, like Roy Rogers, and Gene Autry. Smokey wanted to be a cowboy badly. Every time he went to the movies it was a cowboy-themed movie, so Smokey's uncle started calling him Smokey Joe. The name stayed with him. By the time Smokey was twelve everybody was calling him Smokey, they dropped the name Smokey Joe and just called him Smokey. I have the same problem, everybody calls me by the name that my aunt gave me, not the name that my mom gave me at birth. I mean everybody calls me the name that my aunt gave me all through grade school till present. I can relate to Smokey. His real name is William Robinson Jr.

When Smokey got into the money he earned as a writer, singer, and produce, he tried to make a movie, I'm not sure if it was a cowboy movie, but if you had a chance to talk with Smokey he would tell you that was one of the most financial mistakes he ever made.

As I mentioned before Tamla Records started on January 12, 1959 since Berry received money from the recordings that were hit, he decided to further expand into the business and follow his dreams. As I remember from the start, Berry borrowed $800.00 from his family. Berry's wife Raynoma Singleton (maiden name) had to look for a building she was part of in the company. She found a little house in the new house, it had a big picture window in front. How were all those fabulous recordings coming out of that little house? Let me give you the rundown of this building; the house had an attached garage; Berry and Raynoma lived upstairs. Downstairs is where the offices were, and the kitchen was torn out and turned into the control room; you must have a control room and equipment to operate a recording studio. A big piece of glass was put in the garage to divide the control room from the recording studio. After the proper installation of sound and wiring, the garage area became the recording studio. Berry had a dream where ordinary people could walk through one door and come out the other door a star, plus a factory to produce hits, Berry was bold enough to label his building Hitsville U.S.A. From that point, history was in the making. In 1960, a new label was created. It was blue, and it was called Motown.

Many singers and acts were coming to Motown.

It was an opportunity for people living in low-income projects, such as Smokey Robinson, Diana Ross, Mary Wilson, Aretha Franklin, etc.

For a much better chance to start a new lifestyle.

Motown was unique and quite different. Everyone was coming to Motown; Berry would change some people's and singing groups' names because it did not sound right for an artist. Mary Wells was Motown's first Major recording artist.

She was Ms. hit maker. I remember she was singing to the top of her voice, screaming forcefully. The song she sang was called Bye Bye Baby, a great one. Smokey had ideas about Mary Wells when he heard another side to Mary Wells's voice. He molds her into something different from Bye Bye Baby's lead voice.

He made her sing a little smoother and softer. Smokey added a calypso sound to Mary Wells. That sound came from Harry Belafonte's style of singing. Hits were born.

Like old standby, you beat me to the punch, two lovers; my guy, Smokey, had her under lock and key. One of the unique things was that whenever a writer-producer made a hit on a singer, he or she got a chance to produce the same singer again. However, if the song and the singer do not make a hit, you must let the singer go so another producer gets a chance to produce that singer. Smokey had locks on Mary Wells. Also, he had locks on the Temptations. That means Smokey was always writing hits for Mary Wells and The Temptations. I remember Smokey wrote a song for the Temptations called Get Ready. That song did not do so well, so Smokey had to move aside for Norman Whitfield to have a chance at The Temptations. Norman Whitfield wrote Ain't Too Proud to Beg for the Temptations, that song just pushed Smokey out in the left field for the moment. Every writer and producer were competing. The competition outside was automatic, but inside Motown, it was a task to create those hits. Another unique thing about Motown was quality control, which means every song was voted on before it was released to the public. It was a group of people that consisted of writers, producers, and singers. Berry would play the recording (a demo) and everyone in that group listened. Berry would ask their opinion and use their experience to say whether the recording was a hit or not. If that recording did not get a favorable vote, it was not released to the public. On the other hand, the recordings that were voted favorable and released to the public made it to the charts as a hit usually.

Remember this: when you hear Mary Wells sing, you can hear Smokey's style. If, like Smokey was singing the song, which is how he molded Mary Wells, you could say the song has Smokey's flavor.

In addition, Mary Wells' background voice was The Temptations. The Supremes signed on Motown.

They used to leave school to head to Motown. They were not singing at first, but they would give support to other singers by clapping hands or something of that nature. Berry called them the girls at that time. Martha Reeves was a secretary for Motown before she was a singer. Her group, the Vandellas, were hit makers also; their hits were Come Get These Memories, Dancing in the Streets, and Jimmy Mack, My baby loves me. It took a very long time for the Supremes to get a hit record and also took a very long time for The Temptations to get a hit record, but Berry did not give up on them because he knew what the group could do because of his insight, and he knew the Temptations and the Supremes had that magic and he wanted the world to see it. Their first recording for the Supremes was, I Want a guy 1961. There were four members of the Supremes at first, and the fourth member was Barbara Martin. She had a baby and had to leave to be a mom. Their second single was Buttered Popcorn 1961; the First hit was Lovelight charted #23 in 1963; in addition to other hits, Where Did Our Love Go, Stop In The Name of Love, Baby Love, The Supremes was a Hit machine.

Let me tell you about Steviand Hardaway Morris. You people know him as Stevie Wonder.

Stevie Wonder was discovered by Ronnie White. Ronnie White was one of the Miracles. In addition, Ronnie White helped write the Temptations hit My Girl with Smokey Robinson. Stevie Wonder was introduced to Berry when he was about 7 years old, and it was like an audition for Berry. Stevie was moving his head back and forth while he was talking to Berry. Stevie tried singing a little bit. Berry was not impressed because of the sound of Stevie's voice, so Stevie started playing the bongos plus the drums. Berry said he was not looking for any drummers. He was not impressed. Stevie started playing the piano. Berry said he was good; there was nothing special about it. The fact of the matter is that Berry did not want any little kids on his label at that time. So, when Stevie started to play his harmonica, Berry was excited and extremely impressed with Stevie. Berry signed him on, and at the same time, he changed Stevie's name from Stevland Hardaway Morris to Little Stevie Wonder. He was 7 years old. Stevie's first hit was Fingertips Pt 1 and 2 1963, Berry did not want any more young singers aged ten or eleven.

He was twelve years old when he did fingertips. Also, he had another hit recording, You Are the Sunshine of My Life, signed seal delivered, Isn't She lovely, I Just Called To Say I Love You; Stevie was fabulous. Stevie Wonder co-wrote Tears of a Clown with Smokey Robinson in addition Stevie Wonder Co-producing Minnie Riperton's album in 1974, Perfect Angel. Motown had lots of talented people. They started as singers but decided to work behind the scenes as writers and producers. Some of them, Take Barrett Strong who recorded the song Money on Tamla Records in 1959, and it was a classic. It was the 8th single to be released. Barrett Strong and Norman Whitfield wrote Just My Imagination for The Temptations in 1971. Eddie Holland was a great

11

writer and producer, he and his brother. However, Eddie Holland recorded a record namely Jamie 1961. Brian Holland is his brother. Eddie Holland went behind the scenes to write with his brother. Also, Lamont Dozier was part of the writing team, for Tamla/Motown; there were many more writers.

Motown was on the roll in the right direction, more singers were coming to Motown. In 1964 the Four Tops signed with Motown. The four tops were no strangers to singing. They had already experienced it when they signed with Motown, overall, they have been together for over four decades. They were on chess records for a while, and Columbia records for a while. The four tops started singing together between 1953 and 1954. Their first hit with Motown was Baby I Need Your Loving which was during 1964. The second hit for the Four Tops was Ask the Lonely which was in 1965. The Four Tops was on the roll. The Four Tops were the most consistent hit makers plus original group personnel.

The Temptations was signed in March 1961 in Motown; they auditioned live in front of Berry. The members at that time were Aldrich Bryant, Eddie Kendricks, Paul Williams, Otis Williams, Melvin Franklin. and other writer and producer singers; the name of the song was Mother of Mine. The lead was Paul Williams. Many people would always ask me about Melvin's nickname Blue. They would ask what it means. Is it his favorite color or what? So, I told them. Melvin was inspired by another singer. The singer's name was Domenico Modugno. He recorded a song in 1958 called VOLARE, it was a very unique song Melvin loved the song and the artist because it sounded good and different. Some of the lyrics were NEL BLU DIP IN TO DI BLU Volare means (fly) way up to the sky so Melvin was called Blue because of his inspiration with that song and the singer was Italian.

Berry was impressed because of the singing, choreography, and style. The group was unique. Their first single was a national hit on the chart; however, it made the public listen more to the group. It was #22 in 1963, and the song's name was a dream come true. Eddie Kendricks was singing the lead. How it all started was, a group called the Primes and the Primettes, the Primes were Paul Williams' and Eddie Kendricks'.

The Primittes were Diana Ross Mary Wilson and Florence Ballard when the primes and the Primittes broke up.

The Primes got together with another group, The Distance. They were going to use the name the Elgin's to audition when they came to Motown, the fact of the matter Motown already had a group called the Elgin's, they had a record out called Darling Baby. So, Paul Williams came up with the name Temptations Paul which was deeply religious; Temptations is the word from the Bible.

For the first 3 years, The Temptations had it rough, no-hit record in sight. I remember Paul was going to quit when he stood in front of the Motown building saying how many kids he had, and one was on the way. He wanted to have some kind of job because it was that bad. Smokey said he had an idea that might work. So, Smokey started teaching the new song to the Temptations. The group got upset and full of frustration and said they did not want nursery rhymes (You Could Have Been a Candle You Got a Smile So Bright Sweep Me off My Feet) some of the temps said what kind of a song is that? They needed a song badly, As the temptations started putting the voices together with harmony, they began to like the song. So, the group recorded the song Jan 1964 Smokey Robinson and Bobby Rogers of the Miracles wrote it. The song was called The Way You Do the Things You Do. US Cash Box R&B Single #1 The Temptations first hit.

Everyone was happy about that. Smokey said he had another song for the Temptations. Smokey was going to record the song with his group The Miracles, but he needed that dynamic lead voice of David since he heard him sing. So, the temptations recorded the song. The song was called My Girl released on Jan 21, 1964, that was the Temptation's first million seller which made #1, the rest was history. As a matter of fact, at that time My Girl was the biggest hit for The Temptations it made it to the Grammys Hall A Fame which is an outstanding achievement. Many hits followed such as Ain't Too Proud to Beg, Let Me Tell You about Ain't Too Proud to Beg. It was written by the late Norman Whitfield. Norman was a great writer, he and Smokey were always competing with each other when it came to the Temptations. After My Girl Smokey wrote a song called Get Ready It was ok but not good enough it didn't do that well on the market. So Smokey had to move aside and let Norman Whitfield take a shot at the Temptations. That was one of the rules that the writer who wrote the last song and it was a hit, he or she had another chance to write another song for that same artist. He wrote Ain't Too Proud to Beg for the Temptations blew Smokey out in the water because it was a hit. Something else about that song Ain't Too Proud to Beg, the lead was David Ruffin. The song was way too high the key David had a very hard time recording the song in the studio. Sweat was coming down his face his shirt was all wet, it took a while for David to finish the song. When you hear the song on the radio you can hear David's voice crack not hitting the note full it is the first note. Norman was asked many times to bring the key down a little. Norman says if he had to change the key to that song he might as well throw it away because it wouldn't be a hit. He was right. Norman wrote Just My Imagination Papa Was a Rollin Stone. Papa was a rolling stone Norman refused to change the date on the song. The date was one of the lyrics (it was the 3 of September the beginning of the song. The date was the actual date that the lead voice

Dennis Edwards's Father died. Temptations recorded the song anyway after trying to get Norman to change the date Norman said he was not changing anything the song was a big hit, and Norman was right again plus there were many changes in personnel for the Temptations. Berry had an idea; he recorded the Supremes and the Temptations together. It was successful. Lots of people have asked what makes The Temptations so unique and different. First, let me give you an example so you can really understand.

Back in the 50's you had the Platter's Tony Williams was the lead voice of that group, you heard The Teenagers, Frankie Lymon was the lead voice of that group, The Imperials, and Little Anthony was the lead voice of that group. What did the groups have in common was only one lead voice? Those singing groups mostly stood around a microphone and sang. They were great singers. Why were the Temptations so different? The Temptations had five lead voices and every lead voice could hold his own. They were fabulous and knew how to take care of business, in addition, they just did not stand around a microphone and sing like the other groups who had just one lead voice. The Temptations had to dance, and they were incredibly good at it. I talked to members of the Temptations in the past. I was able to gather information firsthand regarding Motown. Something else was remarkably interesting. You had to be between 5ft 10 in to 6 ft. 2 to sing in the Temptations group, plus your weight had to be in proportion with your height. You had to be able to sing everyone's part in the group and also had to have good looks. Another thing for sure, there would never be a name in front like David Ruffin and the Temptations or Paul Williams and the Temptations, etc. The Temptations was one unit. How did they move so smoothly and with great precision? Give Cholly Atkins all the credit who did the choreography. Also, Lon Fontaine, both were one of a kind. Cholly Atkins guided all the singers with dance steps in Motown and other artists on other labels, we called him POPs. As I said Lon Fontaine also did choreography for The Temptations, he was incredibly good too. Paul Williams and Cholly Atkins used to disagree on lots of steps sometimes, but overall, The Temptations was exceptionally smooth and quite different. In addition, The Temptations gave Motown its very first Grammy award. (David Ruffin was replaced during that time). The song was released on 25th October, 1968, the title was Cloud Nine, Dennis Edwards was the main lead voice. At the end of that song, the other lead voices did their part.

Gladys Knight and the Pips have been around a long time, since 1954. They came to Motown very experienced. Gladys Knight and the Pips are related to Gladys Knight's brother and cousin. She started singing at age seven when she was with other labels. She is a great singer and down to earth. Her brother Baba was a professional dancer. Disc Jockey wrote her first song before coming to Motown. It was a hit. I used to listen to that disc Jockey on the radio when I was a kid. His name was Johnny Otis. He also had a hit record called Willie and the Hand Jive. I always thought he was an afro American by the way his voice sounded, and the way he talked on the radio. The fact of the matter was he was a white person who did a lot for black singers. The name of the song Gladys Knight recorded was called With Every Beat of My Heart. That was in 1961. Johnny Otis did it first.

Gladys Knight and the Pips signed with Motown in 1966. They were ready for the challenge. Gladys Knight and the Pips' first big hit was I Heard It Through the Grapevine in 1967. It went to #1 on the R&B chart and #2 on the pop chart. During the 6 years at Motown, she had other hits, If You Were My Woman, Neither One of Us, Nitty Gritty, she was on the roll. She and her group were nothing but class and she was always sweet as one can be.

Since we are talking about the Grape Vines and Motown's driving force, let me tell you about Marvin Gaye. I went to his house once when you walked in. He had a grand piano right in the living room. He was one of a kind, quite different. Multi-talented, where in the world did this man come from? Meaning what group? During the early 50s there was a singing group with a vastly different harmony style and the name of that group was The Moonglows. One of the lead voices was Bobby Lester and another lead voice was Harvey Fuqua. I spoke with Harvey on many occasions when we both lived in Las Vegas. He gave me lots of information on Motown's early days, firsthand information.

The Moonglows had records on the radio such as See Saw, When I'm with You, Sincerely, 12 Months of the Year, and the 10 Commandments of Love. The lead voice on that recording was Harvey Fuqua. And sometimes Bobby Lester. They were an incredibly good singing group. The young Marvin Gaye was part of that group, Harvey was extremely impressed with his voice and style. When the Moonglows broke up, Harvey Fuqua headed to Motown, and he took Marvin Gaye with him. Harvey collaborated with the artists developing sound and section, at Motown. Marvin was behind the scenes as a house drummer meaning he played drums behind many artists such as Stevie Wonder, The Supremes, The Marvelettes etc,. He was looking to break into the business with Motown. How did anyone at Motown know that Marvin Gaye could sing? It was a house party where Marvin was singing and playing the piano when Berry heard him, it was Berry's house, and he was impressed. Marvin made his first release with Berry, called Let Your Consciences Be Your Guide in 1961. Marvin kept writing for other artists. Finally, in 1962 he had his first hit record called Stubborn Kind of Fellow. Martha and the Vandellas were the background vocals on that recording. He had many more followers, and Motown always accommodated their singers.

How? A group could be recording and need another voice from another group or person they would fill in to help each other. Berry also expanded his ideas to put singers together like The Temptations and The Supremes. He put great singers together as a duet. I remember Kim Weston signed on to Motown in 1963 she had a minor hit called Love Me All the Way and some other songs. However, Berry had decided to put miss hit maker Mary Wells with Marvin Gaye, they recorded What's the Matter With You Baby 1964. Mickey Stevenson was the writer of the song. It was a hit. Mickey Stevenson was a great writer for Motown. I remember Kim Weston's Love Me All The Way in 1963, I mentioned that earlier.

Mickey Stevenson is her husband. Mickey wrote another song, but this time Berry put Kim Weston and Marvin Gaye together on this song, Motown would always be reaching out to do something different with different singers. The song was recorded in 1967 it was called It Takes Two, an excessively big hit. Motown was extremely excited about how the duets were making hits. Motown wanted to do more duets after Kim Weston and Marvin Gaye did so well. Other writers and producers in the Motown circle were watching it also. A husband and wife writing team was looking to record more duets. Unfortunately, Kim Weston was not happy with Motown for some reason and did not realize her song with Marvin Gaye, It Takes Two was going up the chart amazingly fast to be a big hit; Kim Weston left the record company Motown and went to another record company called MGM Records. I believe Berry needed someone to sing with Marvin Gaye in a duet. An incredibly beautiful young lady Berry discovered and signed in 1965, was Thomassina Winfield Montgomery. Berry did not like the name even though it was her legal name. Berry knows best so he changed her name because it was too long and did not fit her as a singer. Motown changed her name to Tammi Terrell. Tammi was an experienced singer who sang on James

Brown's Label King Records (record company). She recorded a song called I Cried, as James Brown's background singer, The Famous Flames was the background vocal on that song, before that James Brown label she recorded with another label song called If You See Bill Very Pretty song. Tammi was looking for that break (note: while she was on James Brown's label they were dating). I do not want to mock anyone, but she could have done much better, there was no appreciation there with James.

It did not last, Tammi left him. That was a good move. When she left, James Brown was so upset and hurt he wrote a song about her. It was a million-seller, it was called I Lost Someone. I met James Brown in the 70s, and I asked about that song because it was so unique, and James Brown told me the story. When any guy sees Tammi Terrell, that song speaks for itself. In addition, she was dating David Ruffin, a bad choice from The Temptations. That was another unique thing about Motown, all the artists dated each other. Nicholas Ashford and Valerie Simpson, husband and Wife wrote as a team for Motown in 1967, they put a song together called Ain't No Mountain High Enough, the song was for Tammi Terrell and Marvin Gaye. I remember Gladys Knight talking to Tammi, Tammi was so excited she was going to sing with Marvin Gaye, she told Gladys she was extremely nervous and Gladys told her she would do simply fine. My friend was right. When Tammi Terrell signed with Motown, she just turned 20 years old, an exceptionally beautiful young lady.

Motown recorded the duet Marvin Gaye and Tammie Terrell the song was called Ain't No Mountain High Enough it was a hit Marvin and Tammie recorded another called Precious Love plus another called Build My Whole World Around You. I believe Kim Weston would have been singing with Marvin Gaye if she had not left Motown. Kim Weston giving the idea to do a duet with Marvin Gaye paved the way for Tammie Terrell to do a duet with Marvin Gaye because the idea made hits. Later on, Marvin did a duet with Diana Ross in the 70s. Motown is still on the roll and was recorded by Marvin Gaye, I heard through the Grape Vine in 1968 that he had numerous hits such as Hitch Hike Ain't That Peculiar, Distance Lover What's Going On which Gladys Knight and the Pips recorded in 1967. I Heard it through the Grape Vine, Marvin recorded the same song in 1968; amazing, both were monster hits. However, Marvin Gaye's recording of Heard Through the Grapevine was the biggest hit between the PIPs and Marvin. Smokey Robinson and Miracles did the song first. That is how Motown works. Try a little of everything to get that hit record on the chart. As I mentioned before, Berry did not want any kids of the label (record company). Diana Ross introduced five kids to sing for Berry but this time he liked what he was hearing because this kid sounded like Frankie Lymon, an incredibly young kid with a great voice. They were the Jackson 5. I knew the Jackson 5 through their father Joe Jackson. The Jackson 5 was signed in 1968. Some of the public only knew that Janic Jackson and Latoyla were the only sisters in the family but there was an older sister, her name was Rebbie Jackson, and she was a great singer. She recorded a couple of songs Centipede and Faithfully Yours. She was very good. Motown had a special section called the corporation that partly consisted of nothing but writers for different singers. Berry recorded the Jackson Five in October 1969, a song called I Want You Back, their first single, however, the Jackson 5 recorded their first song on another label called Steel Town, the song was called Big Boy, but I Want You Back was recorded on the Motown label, and took off to the top of the chart. Gladys Knight and the Pips were going to do the song first, and Diana Ross was going to try. But Berry wanted new talent out there, so the song went to the Jackson 5, they were a phenomenon, let me put it in slang: they were a hit machine everywhere. Songs like I'll Be There, Dancing machine, ABC, The Love You Save, I'll Be There, Maybe

Tomorrow, Looking Through the Window and many more. Berry was walking around with a big smile on his face that could not come off. Motown had another exceptionally beautiful young lady, not Tammie Terrell, Tammie is beautiful too. The singer is Brenda Holloway, I had a crush on her. She was so different in attitude, she had the looks, voice, and everything else was genuinely nice. The thing about Motown was they looked for something special in the singer and Berry had the knowledge to pull the special something out.

Brenda Holloway signed with Motown in 1963. She was 17 years old, the problem was she lived in Los Angeles. Berry was putting together a staff in Los Angeles. A lot of singers did not realize Berry had his eye on the West Coast. However, Brenda Holloway was the first singer to sign a contract with Berry on the West Coast. It will become a reality that Motown and the West Coast will be inseparable. Brenda Holloway had a few hit records between 1964 and 1965 songs such as Every Little Bit Hurts, I'll Always Love You, What Are You Going to Do When I'm Gone, operator. However, she recorded every little bit of hurt earlier with another company. She also co-wrote a great song called You Made Me So Very Happy, by Blood Sweat, and Tears recorded that song. It was a big hit. Let me tell you one thing for sure, Motown was very precise, it did not seem that way because every one of the singers seemed to have a goal and Berry could see that. Here is an example so you can understand. The Spinners have been around since their high school days, in 1951 they have been trying to lay a hit in the charts without success. The group was a failure, Bobby Smith was the original lead voice for the group. As I mentioned earlier, Harvey Fuqua was a great singer and writer and producer. Harvey and his girlfriend wrote a song for the Spinners called That's What Girls Are Made of in 1961, it was on a different label, sub label of Motown, Harvey's girlfriend was Berry's sister—the founder of Motown. The Spinners came to Motown with

Harvey, in 1964 the spinner signed with Motown, a label that was part of Motown. For some reason, Berry did not give the spinners much attention. The spinner was unhappy they just could not get it together; another singing group called the Commodores signed with Motown between 1971 and 1972. The members of the group attended the Tuskegee Institute in Alabama. They got together because two groups had broken up so each member from the former group got together. The names of the two groups were The Mystics and the Jays. They started playing around various places just to find GIRLS. At that time, they still did not have a name yet. The members of the band are as follows: Williams King-trumpet, Thomas McClary-guitar, Ronald LaPread-bass, Walter Clyde Orange-drums, Lionel Richie-saxophone, Milan Williams-keyboard. The group was searching high and low to find a suitable name for themselves. The more they play someplace the more desperate they got. Finally, Walter Clyde Orange, the drummer gave a dictionary to Williams King, the trumpet player, and told him to hurry and find a name for the band. He picked the name The Commodores. The rest was history, the band started playing in their area which included Tuskegee, Montgomery, and Birmingham. They were discovered in New York City— a place called Smalls Paradise. The owner did not like them, he said the band did not have what it takes. However, due to a cancellation, the owner called the Commodores back to play and the band started rolling. They opened for the Jackson 5 and the rest was history.

Lots of singers and groups were coming to Motown while the company grew. The dreadful thing about it was that everyone did not make it. Some got a record deal, and some did not. The recording business is unique, many people do not understand the nature of what goes on behind the scenes. Motown made it into the history books. I believe the world looks at it this way: the poor are struggling trying to get a singing contract, singing for anyone that can get you out of the poor house. People with talent discover Motown, they walk in with their shoes run over poor. The next thing you know, they come out of Motown a star; history in the making. Let me try to give you an insight into how recordings were conducted back in the 60s.

The recording studios did not have all this digital technology and special effects like they do today. When you had to record you had to practice and learn that song which took hours to get it right. Also, the sound had to be right, producers would see to that. Motown had a school for each singer. Single artist groups.

The school was to teach individual people how to talk properly, how to walk, and how to hold a knife and fork.

The majority of the singers and groups came out of high school and lived in the projects (Low-Income Property) and never got a chance to live in an upper-class environment. They had to be taught to be around upper-class people and places. When people saw the acts (singing groups) the world thought the group were natural dancers and the public went wild. The fact of the matter is no one could dance!!!

As you recall I mentioned the choreographer was the key person responsible for the group dancing.

Besides grooming the artist in the school, the artist worked on their steps twelve or more hours a day.

It was hard practicing over and over with the choreography but in the final act of learning the steps, it paid off big time. The teacher for the school was Max. She was a lady who was very classy. When a group or a single artist had to record, the producer would pick the best voice for the song, it depended on what type of song it was to determine the lead voice. Berry would also participate in the same manner; he would choose what song would fit the voice. Sometimes a single artist would sing and need backup voices.

It would be the other groups with Motown that would back up the single artist.

I would like to share some of my perspectives and views regarding recordings and studios. I have been in and out of recording studios all my life.

Today when you see on your television somebody singing in a video, they sound great and moving in different directions, especially a singing group or someone playing an instrument of some type. Do not be disappointed because no one ever sings live, it is all lip-synced every word. However, when they have to do a live show, they have to sing. Some artists try to cheat and lip-sync on a live show. Some of them got caught doing that. Let me talk about recording the lip-synced in the studio you have the control room, the room is mostly divided by a huge glass that is between the control room and the studio where the singer is going to be singing. The singer is on the other side of the glass. In the studio, you can have a large band or orchestra with many members all at once with the singer if he chooses to, and if the studio is large enough, it is up to the producer. The control room is where the engineer sits and looks at you through the window with a microphone to talk with you. Plus, he sits at the control board which is called a mixing board. I will explain to you later. Some people wonder how the singers are paid.

The singers are called artists, singing groups single artists. They are paid what their singing contract calls for. You receive a percentage from the sales of your recording, it is called royalties. Back in my days, it would start with a penny for each copy or two cents, depending on what your contract called for. Today it is much more... The fact of the matter is you made your money going on the road which means performance, on a TV show or live performance in front of a live crowd. TV shows like Johnny Carson show, Soul Train Show, American Bandstand Dick Clark, etc. that is where the money was. The bigger your name, the bigger the check. However, you would have to have a manager to manage the part. On the road was extremely hard going from state-to-state and city-to-city packing and changing into different clothes, it was tough but if you wanted to earn a living, you got on the road. Sometimes you felt sick or did not feel good or you were tired, and your voice sounded tired. But you cannot tell the public who paid to see you, that you are feeling bad, or you have a cold and are tired. When you signed that contract to appear to perform, remember the show must go on!!! Regardless. Let me tell you where the big money is. The writer of the song that made a big hit, the writer gets a much larger percentage of the recording depending on the contract, the percentage can start from 30% to 50%. You want to be a writer in the music business, you have money is much better and easier. However, you need someone to produce the song that was written. The producer is just not a person walking around in the streets. The producer must have an ear and understanding of the sound of the recording. He will select who has the better voice for a certain song if is a singing group with 3 or four lead voices He will determine the best lead for the song the producer calls the shots and works closely with the recording engineer the producer pays for the recording of the song he also received a percentage from, the recording the range could be 20% to 30% depending on the contract. How do you know your recording is selling well? When you get lots of airplay on the radio, you have an organization that tracks your recording when it is played on the air or in a movie or advertising. The organization is called BMI and Ascap The organization receives a report from radio stations or wherever your recording is playing plus you have a magazine, another organization called Billboard also tracks your recording, your song could be in the top

500, top 50, top 25 or top 10, all the way up to number 1. The closer to the top of that magazine the more money you will be making and more popular you will get.

Lots of people always ask how different artists were discovered back in my day. A group could be singing on a street corner hoping someone would be listening in the music business or knew someone in the business to come along. Sometimes people sing at someone's private party and get discovered. The singer would go on a talent show to be discovered, there are so many ways, I was asked one day what the parts of a singing group of five people, how the voices work. I started with the bass voice which is the timekeeper of blend with a bottom sound then you have the baritone. It sometimes calls the off note of the group, he blends the two tenors together making them ring like bells, you have the 2nd tenor, he holds the harmony together, you have the 1st tenor who rounds out the harmony making it complete. Sounds very pretty. The last voice is the lead voice. He carries the group to stardom. Back in my time, it was usually one lead voice like Little Anthony the Imperials, Frankie Lymon, The Teenagers, Tony Williams The Platters, etc. As time moved on groups had more than one lead voice, it was much better.

Over the years, people started producing their own music, getting their own label and recording studio.

In the music business, you hear of artists selling a million copies; these are some of the artists who sold over a million records: Elvis Presley 139 million, The Eagles 120 million, Led Zeppelin 122.5 million.

Michael Jackson has 89 million, and the list goes on. Lots of people do not know where the statement a million seller comes from and where it first started. The very first million-seller was in the year 1902. According to Guinness World Records, the legendary opera singer Enrico

Caruso. His version Vesti la giubba from the opera Pagliacci in 1902. Some of the artists who sold the most ever, 2023 present not included.

The Beatles sold 600.00 million, Elvis Presley 500 million, Michael Jackson 400 million, Elton John 300 million.

At that time period who sold more Elvis Presley or Michael Jackson, it went like this. Second to Elvis Presley in the most physical copies sold is Frank Sinatra with 95,250,000 units sold, coming in third.

Michael Jackson 79,350,000 physical units were sold, and 27 million vinyl's of Thriller were included.

The first million-seller on a CD Dire Straits in 1986 were Brothers in Arms.

How much does an artist get when starting out? Remember I said it depends on the contract deal?

The royalty starts at a low of about 10%, which is a common simple royalty deal. If a CD sells for 15.00 and the royalty deal is 10%, the singer will get $1.50 for each CD. If your album sells a million copies you are supposed to get $1,500,000. It depends on whatever deal you make with the company, which is why you must understand the contract.

The funny thing about music is that everybody wants to sing boxers, comedians, movie stars, etc. The problem is that the majority of them want to sing and cannot, but they try. That is why Motown was different.

People who came to Motown from all over the city and try. When people came to audition it was not just one person to hear them, it was other people's writers, singers, and producers who had already recorded for Motown and had a name in the marketplace. They judged the new singing acts. And these people had recordings out on the market already. What makes a good record marketable? Many factors count, such as the writing, when it comes to writing it is not necessary to rhyme a song, what is necessary is meaning, what is the song about or who? Heartbreaking experience? Or love someone with all your heart. In other words, a relevant story. You have a style of smooth singing or happy sound, ballad. The other factor that gets the public attention is being different. It could be how a lead voice is so different with a beautiful sound pitch singing falsetto that was different back in my days.

Something different like a singing group ages 8 to 11 years old and they sound much older until you see them differently, that is what made Motown so unique, the sound was different from other record companies; they had a backbeat which means the drums were always sounding in the back of the band. But Motown drums backbeat the sound of the drums upfront you could always identify the sound coming from Motown. The public can make you or break you. As I said, being different was the key to getting public attention. Let me give you a perfect example, take the Temptations. Before the Temptations, there were other groups with great singers and great songs but the other groups were just like all the other groups standing around a microphone and singing. One lead voice.

The public went crazy when the Temptations made their appearance with what the public witnessed.

The group was singing, everyone was singing, then the lead voice stepped away singing away from the group. When the next song came around, there was another lead voice who started to sing, and the public was blown away, that's what got the audience excited. The group was moving and stepping into a routine together step by step. Everyone was the same height. Every song that the group sang they were moving together not just standing around a microphone but moving together. Being different is effective. Also, writing a song can be a protest song take Marvin Gaye, the song What's Going On means what is happening in the world people, protesting against lots of things. The public listens because it is brought to their attention and most importantly it is different.

Sometimes a group sings a song, and it plays over the radio, the lead singer sounds exactly like a female.

Because the falsetto was perfect and smooth, in addition, when you heard a singing group sing a song, the lead, it sounds like one person singing, but it was four different voices sharing the song, and when the public saw that, they just went wild because the public thought it was one lead singing, the song was different. I was really surprised that no one nicknamed Smokey Robinson the king of falsettos. Whoo, Baby Baby, You Can Depend On Me, Bad Girl, when you heard him singing those songs, you would think it was a lady singing the songs. That is what it was all about, good music by different styles. Rap music changed the market for sound. The rappers were quite different, and this is why they were so successful because it was so different. The first rappers in History were Kool Herc and Coke, a Rock in April 1955. They laid the foundation for Hip Hop, starting in 1973. It took off something different, it was Hugh. I point out that's how Motown was hugely different and took off. It was Hugh. That is why it is so important to do something different because the Public can make you or break you. Motown was on a roll, with hits all over the place. You have to give Smokey Robinson lots of credit because of Berry's experience and Smokey's.

Willing to listen to Berry and write many songs. Motown was moving with success. Motown was doing so well that Berry appointed Smokey Robinson as Vice President of Motown in 1960. That's how good Smokey was. Berry and Smokey always worked together because of

Smokey's songwriting skills. Smokey got tired of sitting behind a desk, so whenever he had a chance, he went out on the road with the Miracles.

Because that was his first love. Berry could hold the business down while Smokey and the Miracles went out to the public, and they were in demand. The fact of the matter, which is a natural fact, is that Smokey Robinson was the King of Motown. Berry acknowledged that, you know, the old saying, what goes up must come down. Motown was not infallible. Let me explain why. In the 60s, Motown was able to have 79 records in the top 8 or 10 on the Billboard 100, during the duration from approximately 1959 to 1969.

In 1967, there was a riot in Detroit. Motown lost some main writers and producers. Holland and Holland was one of the teams because of a pay dispute. Motown was declining. Because they could not produce different singers and acts, the original singers were moved on to new labels (record companies) or had gotten old, passing their prime. Trying to get new artists to fill the shoes of the original artists and acts was challenging, as were time changes and sounds. In addition, a few deaths of key artists brought the mood down with the other artists, such as Tammi Terrell died on March 16, 1970, she sang with Marvin Gaye, and Florance Ballard died on February 22, 1976, Original Supreme, Marvin Gaye Murdered April 1, 1984.

David Ruffin died June 1, 1991, drug overdose lead voice My Girl Temptations, and Mary Wells died July 26, 1992, with her song MY Guy. Most artists were still singing and performing. They were deeply affected, plus Motown was having problems. But everyone was trying to keep it all together, which was difficult. More artists were moving to other labels (companies), but in reality, the 60s could not recapture or reproduce what was.

Was Motown the first black-owned record company?? Lots of people thought it was the first Black-owned.

However, little did they know it was not true. In the year 1921, in Harlem, New York, the first black-owned record company was called Black Swan, Founder and Owner, Harry Pace.

They recorded Blues and Jazz. Some of the artists were Alberta Hunter, Katie Crippen, and Ethel Waters.

Ethel Waters was also in the movies. One of the movies I consider to be a great movie between good and bad. It was called Cabin in the Sky. Over the years, it was doing well; like everything else, it hit rock bottom. 1923, the company was declared bankrupt. In 1924, Paramount Record Label purchased the Black Swan company. The reason it hit rock bottom is because white companies were stealing material songs, etc., from the black company. Back then, black people did not have any rights whatsoever. Who was more successful?? Black Swan record label or Motown record label. Motown by far. It was a new day with better protection and more knowledge.

Motown was struggling. Many of the singers were not getting paid fully, and more singers were shopping around for a new label. Berry wanted out. Berry was extremely ambitious and willing to strive. Berry wanted to go to higher ground. Motown was in the heart of Detroit.

2648 West Grand Blvd Detroit, Mich. People would always ask me what I thought were the best years of Motown records. I say between 1965 and 1968, Motown dominated the billboard charts. I figured it was the greatest success moment. However, all businesses have their difficulties. In some companies, when problems get worse, there is no chance of bouncing back on the hit parade regarding sales, etc. Other businesses cut prices or go on having big sales to recover and if nothing is working, they declare bankruptcy.

When it came to Motown to try to turn the business around, Berry decided to relocate. I do not mean some place in Detroit; Berry had bigger ideas. Berry wanted to move out West, not just any place, but Los Angeles, California. There are lots of places to move to in Los Angeles. Many counties were available, such as Ventura County, Orange County, San Diego County, and Riverside County; within those counties, you have different cities. Berry's choice is Hollywood California. Motown closed its doors in June 1972.

However, it was not such a smooth transition. The musicians, singers, and the staff who ran the offices showed up for work at 2648 West Grand Blvd in Detroit and could not get in because the doors were locked. Motown had offices earlier in 1963 in the Los Angeles location Sunset and Vine right on the corner. Plus, another office was located in New York during the 60s. The official move to Los Angeles, right in the heart of Hollywood, California, was in 1972. The address was 6255 West Sunset at the corner of Sunset and Argyle. The move to Los Angeles, California, sent a SHOCK WAVE! By the way, in 1967, the Supremes was getting stronger. It was no longer the Supremes; the names were changed officially to Diana Ross and the Supremes. Personally, it was a sad day to change the name since Mary Wilson was a good friend.

After the move, Motown was still trying to recapture the magic they once had. Berry did not give up; he was still looking for something bigger. Motown expanded into making movies. It was a tough business, especially for a newcomer, but Berry was very set in his mind to be part of the new challenge.

Business as usual for the recording. Four months after moving from Detroit, Motown launched a movie. Let me think back. I remember when

Berry met with other movie makers and producers, etc. They could not come to an agreement of some type. The other mover maker had the movie, and somehow, Berry didn't like what was said. Berry cussed at that person saying give me my @#$%# film. Berry was incredibly determined to make the film; it was about a jazz singer named Billie Holiday. The song was sung and written by Billie Holiday the year was 1956. The name of the film Lady Sings the Blues, staring Diana Ross. Also, Diana Ross had gotten married in 1971 to Robert E. Silberstein while she was pregnant with Berry's child. Berry had outstanding actors in the film. It was released in October 1972. The film did very well, and it received the NAACP Image Award and Nominations Academy Award, directed by Sidney J Furie, proving that the other companies that were against making the movie were totally wrong. Again, Berry is all smiles.

Berry met the challenge and kept going as much as he could. He did notice times have definitely changed the music and the way it was. He kept trying until one day he woke up. I imagine he said he reached his peak and accomplished many things. Around June 1988, Berry sold his empire Motown Records. I was shocked, but anyway, I thought he had to sell because he had accomplished his goals and challenges; I salute Berry because he was the best and highly creative and a great leader and manager.

He sold Motown for $61 Million to the Music Corporation of America (M.C.A). The move from Detroit to Los Angeles hurt many artists. In Los Angeles, the homes are extremely expensive, have sky-high rent in a decent area, and get used to new surroundings. Lots of things have to be considered. Berry calls it progress. I do not blame him for it because it is his company. All the artists work there. Berry is 94 years old and still going strong.

I have learned many things from Motown. The Temptations, Smokey Robinson, Marvin Gaye etc., we are all good people to know. Berry is just enjoying life, taking it a day at a time at the age of 94. All the Motown acts are up in age from the 60s; some are retired, some have passed on, and some are still doing the best of their ability to go forward. When music is in the blood, you keep going as long as you can, and with God's help. I thank Berry for giving me a chance to experience the Motown sound. There will never be a sound that took the world like the Motown sound, it was in a class of its own. I hope that all the remaining artists have nothing but blessings and guidance. Enjoy life, love one another, and help each other when possible. I feel so blessed that I am a witness, can share what I know regarding the Motown phenomenon. Berry was at the helm and did a fabulous job. He knew. The sound was required for each artist or was it the right type for an artist. I thought I had a good ear, but Berry had a golden ear for music. The Motown school was a great idea. When you came out of that school, you were ready to meet anyone and ready for the road and the world. In today's music I wish them all the best of luck, but they could never be another Motown. Good luck with your life Berry! May God keep blessing you.

And remember, when you pick a Berry from a vine and eat it, you will think about Motown. Because it is a good thing.

P.W. Williams Date April 15, 2024

PW Williams

www.ingramcontent.com/pod-product-compliance
Lightning Source LLC
Chambersburg PA
CBHW081749200326
41597CB00024B/4447